EAT LIKE
A LOCAL-
EDINBURGH

Edinburgh United Kingdom Food Guide

Nathalie Ahmadzadeh

CZYK Publishing Since 2011.
CZYKPublishing.com
Eat Like a Local

Lock Haven, PA
All rights reserved.
ISBN: 9798715184931

BOOK DESCRIPTION

Are you excited about planning your next trip? Do you want an edible experience? Would you like some culinary guidance from a local? If you answered yes to any of these questions, then this Eat Like a Local book is for you. Greater Than a Tourist – Eat Like a Local, Edinburgh, Scotland by Nathalie Ahmadzadeh, takes you beyond the tourist traps of the Royal Mile to discover a palate of flavours and cuisines. Culinary tourism is an important aspect of any travel experience. Food has the ability to tell you a story of a destination, its landscapes, and culture on a single plate. Most food guides tell you how to eat like a tourist. Although there is nothing wrong with that, as part of the Eat Like a Local series, this book will give you a food guide from someone who has lived at your next culinary destination.

In these pages, you will discover advice on having a unique edible experience. This book will not tell you exact addresses or hours but instead will give you excitement and knowledge of food and drinks from a local that you may not find in other travel food guides.

Eat like a local. Slow down, stay in one place, and get to know the food, people, and culture. By the time you finish this book, you will be eager and prepared to travel to your next culinary destination.

OUR STORY

Traveling has always been a passion of the creator of the Eat Like a Local book series. During Lisa's travels in Malta, instead of tasting what the city offered, she ate at a large fast-food chain. However, she realized that her traveling experience would have been more fulfilling if she had experienced the best of local cuisines. Most would agree that food is one of the most important aspects of a culture. Through her travels, Lisa learned how much locals had to share with tourists, especially about food. Lisa created the Eat Like a Local book series to help connect people with locals which she discovered is a topic that locals are very passionate about sharing. So please join me and: Eat, drink, and explore like a local.

TABLE OF CONTENTS

DEDICATION

I dedicate this book to my Nana. She was a fearless woman, who loved going on adventures, had an unbelievable appetite for cake, and always came through when you needed her.

ABOUT THE AUTHOR

Nathalie is a freelance writer, foodie, and film buff based in Edinburgh. She initially moved to Edinburgh to study film in 2014 but fell in love with the city and has remained ever since.

Originally from Sweden and with Iranian heritage, Nathalie is multi-cultured. She's always been curious about the world and has spent years moving around, travelling, and discovering the world. A keen explorer, she loves trying new things. Nathalie particularly loves old cities – another reason she settled in Edinburgh – and finds them an infinite soured of creative inspiration.

While Nathalie predominately writes fiction, she loves sharing her experiences and tips with the people around her. This book attempts to share some of the things that have made her and the people around her fall in love with the Scottish capital.

HOW TO USE THIS BOOK

The goal of this book is to help culinary travelers either dream or experience different edible experiences by providing opinions from a local. The author has made suggestions based on their own knowledge. Please do your own research before traveling to the area in case the suggested locations are unavailable.

Travel Advisories: As a first step in planning any trip abroad, check the Travel Advisories for your intended destination.
https://travel.state.gov/content/travel/en/traveladvisories/traveladvisories.html

FROM THE PUBLISHER

Traveling can be one of the most important parts of a person's life. The anticipation and memories that you have are some of the best. As a publisher of the *Eat Like a Local*, Greater Than a Tourist, as well as the popular *50 Things to Know* book series, we strive to help you learn about new places, spark your imagination, and inspire you. Wherever you are and whatever you do I wish you safe, fun, and inspiring travel.

Lisa Rusczyk Ed. D.
CZYK Publishing

Eat Like a Local

'Eating and drinking wants but a beginning.'

– Scottish Proverb

When I first moved to Scotland, I'll admit it, I thought very little of their food. The mere mentioning of haggis made me cringe as I envisioned a plate filled with intestines. There's a saying about how Scottish people will try to deep-fry anything, and you can easily find chippy shops who will gladly take on that challenge. Mars bars, sausages, pies, pizzas, boiled eggs – you name it, and they'll fry it! But it turned out that beyond the rumours and prejudices, a world of food is available for you to explore. Edinburgh is a growing city, and new places pop up all the time – be it restaurants, shops, or cultural venues.

Compared to gigantic cities like London, Edinburgh is barely a town. But in addition to great culture and history, this walkable city has an incredible diversity of food to offer, if one only knows where to look. Seven years after moving here, I still end up discovering new places to eat almost every week.

This city is known for the Fringe and the cultural explosion that happens every August. But Edinburgh is worth a visit any time of the year, and in this book, I've even included some season-specific tips.

Before we start, let me make something clear. If you visit Edinburgh, the problem won't be finding tasty things to eat – the problem will be limiting yourself from doing anything but eat.

Edinburgh
United Kingdom

Edinburgh
UK
Climate

	High	Low
January	44	33
February	45	33
March	48	36
April	52	39
May	58	43
June	62	48
July	65	51
August	65	51
September	61	48
October	55	43
November	48	37
December	45	34

GreaterThanaTourist.com

Temperatures are in Fahrenheit degrees.
Source: NOAA

1. THE WALKABILITY

First things first. Edinburgh was founded in the 12th century and is amongst the oldest cities in the United Kingdom. The city is pretty condensed and hosts a population of around 500,000 in its metropolitan area. In difference to several other cities of similar size, Edinburgh is very walkable. It'll be a bit of a hike, but it's possible to walk from one end of the city centre to another. The city holds UNESCO World Heritage status and is one out of six World Heritage sites in Scotland. Filled with narrow closes, cobbled streets, and secret passages – there's space for anything and everything. It has resulted in Edinburgh hosting some pretty unique and niched places, with several of them focused on eating.

2. CASH OR CARD?

Easy card paying solutions like iZettle has really changed the number of places that now take card, and other electronic payments. Compared to just a few years ago, you'll find that you can pay with card pretty much everywhere. There are, however, some exceptions and places that require a minimum spending to be able to pay with cards. While it's

13

namely corner shops with this system, there are actually a couple of restaurants worthy of a visit that doesn't take card payments. You absolutely do not need to rely on cash to enjoy your time in Edinburgh, but it can be worth exchanging a smaller amount just to be safe.

3. TO TIP OR NOT TO TIP

If you've ever visited the United Kingdom before, you might be aware that you don't have to tip the way you'd do in, for example, the United States. However, in restaurants and nicer establishments, you should tip about 12% or more if the service has been excellent. Waiting staff doesn't need their tip to survive. Still, as the jobs are often minimum wage, they rely on that extra income. If you don't tip, the staff won't be rude to you. Still, it is considered strange if you have a large, expensive meal and then don't leave any tips.

Be aware that if you're part of a bigger group, it's quite common for restaurants to charge a service fee, which tends to be equal to the tipping amount.

4. THE EARLY MORNING HEROES

Breakfast is a big thing in Edinburgh. There are probably hundreds of different places that specialise in only serving breakfast and, in some cases, lunch. They open early, and they close early. You will find a place that serves breakfast, either for sitting in or takeaway, on pretty much every street of the city, particularly in tourist crowded areas.

Overall, Edinburgh isn't a particularly pricey place to eat out in. Still, breakfast is often incredibly affordable, and you can get a big meal for a small penny. A full Scottish breakfast is similar to a classic English breakfast, with a few differences. You'll always get a tattie scone, a type of fried potato bread, and black pudding, which is a sausage made with blood and oats.

Another popular breakfast dish is Eggs Benedict. Loudons, which now has two city centre locations, specialise in making eggs benedict with various toppings. In addition to their Eggs Benedict, they have an extensive breakfast, brunch, and lunch menu.

If you're staying slightly south of the city centre, there are a couple of hidden gems worth visiting. Piecebox is a little family-run café on the corner of Polwarth. Montpellier in Bruntsfield opens in the morning and shuts at night, so you're able to eat either breakfast, lunch, dinner, or all three. Both of these places are very affordable, and the food is of high quality.

A very cheap eats that's popular with locals is Snax Café. It's by no means a fancy place, but their simplicity doesn't compromise their food quality. You won't find trendy dishes like avocado on toast or poke bowls here, though. Instead, Snax serves up no-nonsense, classic breakfasts – like fry ups, filled rolls, and baguettes.

5. THE CAFFEINE FIX

Let me be completely honest with you. Depending on where you're from, you won't like the standard of coffee in Edinburgh. Overall, the United Kingdom is pretty bad at making coffee. Unless you are looking for hot milk or bland, weak concoctions, stay far away from all the big coffee chains like Starbucks, Café Nero, and Costa.

Is all hope lost then, if you, like me, are addicted to a good cup of coffee? Definitely not. In recent years small coffee places have started to pop up all around the city. While not all of them have an excellent coffee standard, they're definitely the ones to keep an eye out for. Several of them have exclusive beans or even roast their own ones, and they are independent companies. You'll be able to spot them quite easily if you're out exploring.

My absolute favourite place for good coffee is Gordon St Coffee. This Glasgow company roasts its own beans, and I have never had a less than perfect coffee there. The staff is friendly. They have so many regulars that you often come in to find everyone in the café having a group conversation. The one downside to this place is that it's relatively small with few tables, and the metal chairs aren't the most comfortable if you're looking to stay for a while.

Some other coffee places that I'm fond of and highly recommend visiting are Castello Coffee,

Project Coffee, Artisan Roast, Machina Espresso, and Cairngorm Coffee.

While the coffee has recently had an upswing in quality, you've always been able to get a good cup of tea. Everywhere in Scotland, you can find so-called tearooms, and Edinburgh is no exception. Two companies make their very own tea – Eteaket and Pekotea. The latter is more of a shop and takeaway. But Eteaket is a good café with breakfast, lunch, the best chocolate cake in this world, and, of course, a large selection of tea.

Another great tip is to visit Rosevear tea, which sells over 140 different kinds of loose-leaf tea. Just like Pekotea, Rosevear is a shop rather than a café, but the staff is lovely and happy to make you a cup before you decide on buying. They also have delicious brownies, and if you're lucky, they might give you a sample of that for free.

6. LUNCH

In Edinburgh, a typical lunch consists of either a sandwich, some soup, or a combination of both. It's common to find soup and half a sandwich on any menu serving lunch, and it's a great choice if you like me tend to want to eat everything.

Sandwiches, though, are everything for locals. Traditionally referred to as a 'piece,' it's rare to see the older generations eat anything but a sandwich for lunch. Because of this, there are some excellent sandwich places around. Arguably the best one is Peppers Café and Sandwich bar. This place serves fantastic sandwiches with flavoursome fillings, and they're incredibly cheap. You can sit in, but the café is small, and I would definitely recommend considering taking your sandwich with you. The staff is very much no-nonsense and as full of flavour and character as the sandwiches themselves.

Another classic lunch dish suitable for someone on a budget who still wants to get really full is a baked potato. Baked potatoes are so popular that there are places that sell nothing else. A typical filling is beans and cheese, but you'll generally be able to get any filling imaginable.

The Baked Potato Shop of Cockburn Street is a bit of an establishment, and if you're in the city centre, you will no doubt pass it. Their potatoes are big, and they offer about thirty different fillings. However, they do only have one table, so it's definitely more suitable for lunch on the go.

7. JUST CHEESE FOR LUNCH

Meltmongers is a small local chain that specialises in one thing – food covered in cheese. They primarily sell toasties with different kinds of cheesy fillings but also have cheesy burgers, hot dogs, mac and cheese, and fries. They have one location in Bruntsfield and one in Stockbridge. Both close in the afternoon, so you'll need to head there for brunch or lunch.

To this day, Meltmongers make the best mac and cheese I have ever eaten – and I've eaten loads. They do have tables, and it's an okay place for sitting in. But if you're in the Bruntsfield location and the weather is enjoyable, I would recommend getting your food to go, walk across the road and eat it in the Bruntsfield Links – another park in the middle of the city. If you're at their Stockbridge location, there are still some good, picturesque places to go, as the Water of Leith runs all along with it.

8. BAGELS STRAIGHT FROM MONTREAL

Another brunch and lunch shout-out goes to Bros Bagels. Just like Meltmongers, they have one shop in Bruntsfield and one in Stockbridge. They're so popular that they've been expanding rapidly, and you can now also get their bagels in the west end, in Leith, and in Portobello.

Bros Bagels prides itself in making hand-stretched bagels, just like you'd get them in Montreal. They have various hot and cold fillings to suit any craving or diet, such as pastrami, chicken, or beef. They also have a pretty extensive selection of vegan and vegetarian bagels. The fillings can vary between restaurants, but on average, they have about twenty different choices.

9. AFTERNOON TEA

After breakfast and sometimes lunch comes afternoon tea. Afternoon tea, like the name suggests, includes a big pot of tea. But you also get to munch on sandwiches, scones, and an assortment of cakes.

There are many places in Edinburgh that claim to have the best afternoon tea in the prettiest location. However, you might need to choose between the tastiest afternoon tea or the most photo-friendly venue, as no place has mastered both.

I should know; I've been to all of them. My mother is somewhat obsessed with afternoon tea, so each time she comes to visit, we go to a new place. But there's only been one place we go back to time after time – Mimi's Bakehouse on the Shore.

Mimi's is a local baking chain, so you can actually get afternoon tea in some of their more central locations – such as the Royal Mile and Market Street. But the bakery is on the shore, so here you're guaranteed to get the freshest goods. They make a classic afternoon tea, or you can get it with prosecco if you're feeling celebratory.

It's worth noting that afternoon tea is quite pricey for what it is. Mimi's or Eteaket probably has the best value. The Dome has the most negligible value. Somewhere in the middle is the Witchery, which is on the pricier side. Still, it's a beautiful place to eat, everything is high quality, and the service is excellent. There are plenty of other cafés that offer afternoon tea, but always try to go to a place that makes the sandwiches and scones from scratch.

10. A STRONG CAFÉ CULTURE

Everyone in Edinburgh loves going to cafés. May it be for a quick coffee or tea, something to eat or some cake – it's very common to meet up with your friends at a local spot. There's been a swift between the generations, where older people used to always meet up in the pub. Young people still love going to the pub, but today it's as common to socialise over a coffee as it is over a pint. Some cafés have even been forced to have a time limit during certain hours of the day, as the customers simply don't want to leave.

Several of the beforementioned coffee places are also cafés. But there are some other places worth their own mention, especially because of their interior and comfortable seating.

Crumbs, just off Grassmarket, is a café where people tend to spend hours on end. They are known for their excellent cakes, but it's also a great, somewhat tucked away place. Try to get one of the window seats for an extra cosy visit.

Kilimanjaro Coffee in the southside of the city has seating booths as well as ordinary tables. It's very popular and often filled with locals, but the booths do give you a sense of privacy. They serve hot and cold drinks, cakes, and lighter food.

Soderberg is a Swedish café chain that has a couple of locations in the city. Just by the Meadows, they have their biggest café, a bakeshop, and a restaurant specialising in sourdough pizza. Soderberg is inspired by Swedish baking and has some delicious, filling sandwiches. There are ample seating and a perfect place to rest for a couple of hours before continuing on.

The Black Medicine Coffee Company is extremely popular amongst locals. This is the type of place where people go to get a coffee, take a nice seat, and then spend ages studying or working on their laptops. You can easily hide away, and the ambiance is low even if there are many people.

11. BOARD GAME CAFÉS

Board Game cafés have recently popped up all over the city. A perfect way of meeting up with friends, you can have a drink or something to eat while also playing board games. My favourite one is Noughts and Coffees on Morrison Street.

Another board and comic book café staple, Geek Retreat, is due to open in Edinburgh in 2021.

12. A MULTI-CULTURAL CITY

People from all over the world live in Edinburgh, and this is definitely reflected in the food culture. No matter what you're in the mood for, I can almost guarantee that there'll be a restaurant serving it. If you're looking for something more local, head into the nearest pub. Pubs traditionally serve classic Scottish food – like haggis and pies. They overall have a good standard and will also have a good selection of beers and whiskey to accompany your meal.

It would be impossible to go through all the different cuisines you can and should try out on your visit. But I will tell you about some that I believe to be unmissable.

13. UNIQUELY NICHED – RESTAURANTS THAT ONLY SERVES ONE THING

One of these places is the restaurant Wings, tucked away at Old Fishmarket Close. Like the name suggests, this place only serves chicken wings. I was brought here for the first time by my partner, who wanted to see me eat messily with my hands. But don't feel discouraged if you, like me, hate eating meat off the bone. To my partner's disappointment, they do offer a boneless option.

But the real charm to Wings is while they only serve fried chicken and a couple of minor sides is that you've got almost 80 different sauces to choose from for your chicken to be marinated in. With everything from classic barbeque to boozy whiskey flavours, Wings definitely isn't a boring choice. The décor is inspired by various cult TV shows and games. It's an inexpensive place to eat, and it's open from noon until 11PM – so as long as you're not a vegetarian, there's literally no reason for you not to visit.

If you're feeling less like chicken, more like Asian, then head over to Sister Bao in Newington. Just like Wings, they specialise in one thing – bao. If you have never seen the short Pixar film Bao or tasted the goodness of this type of Chinese dumpling, there's no better place for it.

Another place that niches on one dish is Stockbridge Mac and Cheese. In difference to the other restaurants, they only do deliveries. Their mac and cheese is so popular that you may need to plan ahead a couple of days to make their list. But trust me, it's worth it.

14. DINNER WITH A VIEW

Speaking of places to eat that might be more suitable for a special occasion, Edinburgh has several restaurants with breathtaking views. For a truly luxurious experience, try The Lookout by Gardener's Cottage. This restaurant is situated on Carlton Hill, which is a great lookout point by itself. Their menu is seasonal, so it changes frequently.

Another excellent option is Chaophraya. This Thai restaurant offers great views in the middle of the city centre – ask to sit in the glass box or on the terrace – and is suitable for everything from a special occasion to a family meal. While Chaophraya won't be the cheapest eat, it will be affordable.

There are several other places in Edinburgh that can add a great view as part of their appeal. If you're looking to combine food with shopping or exploring in the same building, try Tower Restaurant inside the National Museum of Scotland or Harvey Nichols Fourth Floor Restaurant Brasserie.

An honourable mention also goes out to SKYbar Edinburgh, which is part of the DoubleTree by

Hilton. Should you get peckish, they do serve food, but most people come here to have drinks with a view.

15. FINE DINING

Edinburgh has no less than four Michelin-star rated restaurants if you're looking for something even more special. The Kitchin and Martin Wishart are located by the shores of Leith, a quick bus ride or about half an hour walk from the centre. The shore is a beautiful place to spend a day, with little shops, cafés, and restaurants in every corner. If you're interested in architecture, you can find some very old buildings and churches in the area, dating back to the 14th century.

Number One and Condita are more central, the first one being located inside the Balmoral Hotel and the second one between Old Town and Southside. All these restaurants focus on local, seasonal produce and their menus are generally new interpretations of Scottish dishes and flavours.

16. ADDRESS TO A HAGGIS

I know, I know, haggis doesn't have the best reputation. A sheep stomach filled with sheep's pluck doesn't sound very appetising. But it is a very traditional Scottish meal. The famous poet Robert Burns even wrote a poem in honour of the dish, and every year on Burn's night, it's traditional to eat haggis. It actually took me years before I could stomach to try it, but now I don't only eat but love haggis.

If you order haggis at a restaurant, it's often taken out of the stomach before it's served. The pluck is grounded and mixed with oats and just looks like multicoloured mince. It tastes rich, spicy and hearty, and should be enjoyed with mashed potato, mashed neeps, and sauce.

The proper way to enjoy haggis is to get some from the butcher and cook at home. You can also buy haggis from pretty much any supermarket. These ones are often wrapped in plastic rather than a sheep's stomach, and there are vegetarian versions of it as well.

But as visitors might not always have access to a proper kitchen at their accommodation, here are some eat out options: Whiski Rooms on Bank Street are often considered by locals to be one of the best places for haggis, as is Angels with Bagpipes. They're both located on the ever so famous Royal Mile, and depending on the time of the year, it can be hard to get a reservation. These two might be a slightly pricier option, so another tip is to check if your local pub has haggis. Chances are high that they do.

17. THE APPLE OF MY PIE

In Scotland, pies are predominately savoury. Sweet pastries are called crumbs and aren't encrusted in a pie shell but instead have crumbly bits of dough on top. The savoury pies are not to be underestimated. It's a classic Scottish meal, then served with mash and sauce, an excellent meal on the go, and often a late-night delight after a night out.

Pies come with all kinds of fillings, some less traditional than others – like mac and cheese filling. Steak pie and Scotch pie are the ones you need to try. Again, if you have access to an oven, you'll get the best pies from your local butcher. Otherwise, try Mum's Comfort Food or The Piemaker.

A relative to the pies are sausage rolls. Sausage rolls are common in all of the United Kingdom, but in Scotland, they make a point to fill them with the most imaginative flavours. Sausage rolls aren't particularly healthy, but they're cheap and great if you want something to snack on while walking.

18. A GOOD OLD BURGERS

An ever so popular choice for any dinner is, of course, burgers. While meat has always been a staple in Scottish cuisine, burgers had an upswing in popularity about ten years ago. The trend hasn't gone away, and you now find numerous gourmet burger places that put McDonald's' to shame. If you do want MacDonald's, though, fear not, there are several of those as well.

One of the very best places for burgers is Boozy Cow. The funky name reflects their funky menu, décor, and overall feeling. They are famous for their inventive milkshakes and are, as far as I know, the only place to sell deep-fried pickles, and of course, the burgers are mouth-watering. The site is small and a hybrid between a bar and a restaurant, so it's more suitable for a group of friends than a family with little kids.

19. BLOODY STEAKS

Continuing on the meat trail, one of the most classic dinners – steak. Those that love it knows how hard it can be to find a really good steak. The most well-known one might be Miller and Carter on Frederick Street, and while their steaks are excellent, they're by no means the best. Chop House is another popular choice, which benefits from having two locations – one just off Princes Street and another in Bruntsfield.

But the two best places for steak lie a short walk from Princes Street. The first one, Toro Latino Café and Grill, is a pretty new place, but it's quickly acquired a fan base. The second one is Los Argentinos, located in Newington. If you're craving a full plate of meat, there are no places I can recommend more than these two.

20. FISH AND CHIPS

Fish and chips are as much a thing in Scotland as it is in England. But there's one vital difference, in Edinburgh, and only in Edinburgh, fish and chips are served with brown sauce. Brown sauce is a tangy, vinegar heavy sauce that goes all over your meal. It's both an acquired taste and surprisingly easy to like. If you try it, you'll be sure to miss it once you get fish and chips elsewhere in the world.

21. FOR THE NON-MEAT EATERS

Edinburgh isn't just a city for meat-eaters. Veganism has really grown in Edinburgh in the past couple of years, and restaurants and cafés that only serve vegetarian food are becoming more and more common.

Holy Cow at the top of Leith prides itself with being the first vegan café in Edinburgh. But the other ones to try are Beetroot Savage in Newington and Seeds for the Soul in Bruntsfield. There's also Pumpkin Brown on Grassmarket, specialising in healthy bowls and salads.

For a fine dining experience, try David Bann Restaurant on St Mary's Street. All of their food is either vegetarian, vegan, or gluten-free. There's also Sora Lella Vegan Roman Restaurant. As the name suggests, they specialise in roman food and are the only one of its kind.

22. INDIAN FOOD

You've probably heard that you'll find the best Indian food outside of India in the United Kingdom. While the dishes here have little in common with the stuff you'd eat in actual India, there's nothing better than a warm, spicy curry after a day of exploring. Edinburgh isn't shy of Indian restaurants, and most of them hold a very high taste quality. But don't go to the ones right off Princes Street – with the exception of Kahani at the top of Leith – and instead, check out some of these ones; Tuktuk, Bombay Bicycle Club, Navadhanya, Slumdog, and Mother's India Café.

If you want to go fancy Indian, there's really no other place than Dishoom on St Andrew Square. Suitable for couples, friend groups, and families alike,

Dishoom is slightly pricier than most other Indians but still not unreasonable. They recently released a cookbook, so you even have the option of taking all the recipes home with you.

23. A TASTE OF NAPLES

This tip might be less interesting if you're, in fact, from Naples. But those of us who dream of Neapolitan food can find comfort in that Rosario Sartore has opened up two Neapolitan restaurants. Each of them has a different concept. Locanda de Gusti specialises in seafood and Pizzeria 1926 in pizza. Pizzeria 1926 is perfect for a group of friends or for families. The location is small and uniquely decorated, making you feel like you are, in fact, in Italy. Locanda de Gusti is calmer and suitable for a special occasion or if you're looking for a romantic dinner.

24. MORE PIZZA

There's no way around it; I love pizza. In my life, I don't think I've met anyone who doesn't like pizza. It's easy, versatile, often cheap, transportable, and therefore works for pretty much any occasion.

The quickest kind of takeout pizza you can buy from kebab shops and well-known chains are surprisingly expensive in Edinburgh. Instead, I would recommend going to one of the many Italian restaurants. Here, you'll find excellent pizza, and it'll be cheaper than a Dominos takeout. You don't have to sit in either, so if it's a nice day, order it as a takeout and go enjoy it in parks like the Meadows or Princes Street Gardens.

A couple of tips are Frizzante, Mia, and Civerinos. Civerinos sell both whole pizzas – up to a massive 20 inches – and individual slices, so it's the perfect meal on the go or for a big meet-up.

25. ASIAN GEMS

Just like in most other European countries, you'll quickly find Asian takeaways and buffets. These places have little resemblance to authentic Asian food. However, Edinburgh also hosts some fantastic Asian restaurants that will satisfy any craving you might have. The popularity has soared in recent years, and you can find many specialist places.

Since Asian is a very broad term, I've divided the tips into more chewable categories.

26. HOTPOT

I tried hotpot for the first time in Australia. Needless to say, I was blown away and spent ages trying to find a place that did it in Edinburgh. I eventually found Xiangbala Hotpot, a restaurant in the Dalry area of the city. Xiangbala is a local gem, and there are hardly any tourists there. Most of their customers are Chinese, which speaks for the authenticity and quality. They are still pretty much the only dedicated hotpot place in Edinburgh, but they do it well. There's nothing quite like going for hotpot one a cold, dreary day, which unfortunately Edinburgh has plenty of.

If you do decide to visit, know that they only accept cash. ATMs are just across the road, though, so should you forget, it's easy to fix.

27. KOREAN BBQ

In difference to hotpot, Korean BBQ has been popular in Edinburgh for some time. The experience of cooking your own meat and all of the tasty side dishes makes Korean BBQ perfect for a social dinner. My favourite place is simply called Korean BBQ and is slightly south of the city centre on Tarvit Street.

Another popular place is Ong Gie. My South Korean friend swears it's the most authentic Korean place in all of Scotland, and they make their own kimchi. What's funny is that Ong Gie lies just one street away from Korean BBQ, so should one of them be fully booked, head over to the other. Ong Gie doesn't just have Korean BBQ, so the menu is more versatile. It is classified as fine dining, so it may be more suitable for smaller groups, a date dinner, or a special occasion.

28. THAI FOOD

Whatever part of the city you're in, you'll always be able to find a Thai place nearby. Curries and Pad Thai are ever so popular dishes, and there is everything from fine dining, street food, and takeaways. One of the most popular places is Ting Thai Caravan, which specialises in a few excellent dishes. It started out as a food truck, but they now have two restaurants on Lothian Road and Teviot Place.

In the Bruntsfield area of the city is Thai Lemongrass, which has a more traditional Thai menu. This place is very suitable for families, a proper sit in restaurant, but not too fancy for a regular dinner. Another place is Sprit of Thai, which lies just behind the concert hall Usher Hall. Spirit of Thai is a small place, perfect for a date night, and they serve very authentic food.

29. NOT THE DREAM CITY FOR SUSHI

One of my sorrows in life is that Edinburgh really isn't a sushi city. Sushi is generally considered a posh food, so the places that sell it charge accordingly. There are a few more affordable places, but most of the time, you'll end up compromising on the quality. This doesn't mean that the sushi places are bad. There are some good places, and there are also a couple of good takeaways if you're not up for leaving your accommodation.

So, if you just cannot be without sushi for the duration of your stay, then the places that are good are Kanpai Sushi, Koyama, and Soul Sushi. YO! Is the only place with a sushi train, so it might be worth a visit for that experience and has a great view, but the sushi is so and so. There are also the restaurants Maki & Ramen and Bentoya, both serving a wide variety of Asian dishes, including sushi.

30. DON'T BE AFRAID OF THE BACKSTREETS

Before we move on from Asian food, let me just say this – Edinburgh is a pretty safe city, especially the central parts. You don't have to shy away from backstreets or tiny alleyways in worry of being robbed. In fact, in Edinburgh, you'll find so many little restaurants, cafés, and shops located in these corners of town. While this is something to keep in mind, whatever your goal is, it rings particularly true for Asian food. Little restaurants tend to pop up everywhere. Some stay and others don't, so grab your chance to visit when you see one.

Some of these places include Ikigai Ramen and Korean Restaurant Sodaeng, which you'd never find if you don't deviate from the high street.

31. ROAD TRIP EATS

There are loads of places to go, things to see and stuff to eat in the city centre. But there's just as much outside of it. If you're planning on taking a day where you explore the outskirts of the city, such as

Portobello Beach, Newhaven, or North Berwick, here are some places not to miss.

The Fishmarket at Newhaven Pier. Selling everything from oysters to fish and chips, this place will suit any type of group. My favourite thing to do on a nice day is to cycle down to Newhaven, get a fish and chips to go, and then eat it out on the pier.

The Lobster Shack in North Berwick is a food truck that sells most things seafood and fish, paired with chips and various dips. North Berwick is lovely when the weather is nice, and you can enjoy your food while sitting or walking along the beach.

32. A TASTE OF THE MIDDLE EAST

While Middle Eastern food is way less common in Edinburgh than, for example, Indian or Pakistani food, there are still some excellent places to go should you crave charcoal-grilled meats and vegetables.

33. WHEN YOU CAN'T CHOOSE

Hanam's is famous for locals and tourists alike and is centrally located next to the castle, at the top of the Royal Mile. Their menu is a mix of various Middle Eastern cuisines. In traditional Middle Eastern spirit, they do not serve any alcohol, so if you're craving a glass of wine with your meal, this might not be the place for you.

34. FOR ANYTIME IN THE DAY

Pomegranate sits just at the top of Leith. They serve Middle Eastern meze and lighter dishes, so it's the perfect in-between meals place or if you're looking for something light to eat. Try their hummus. Trust me on this.

35. PERSIA MEETS LEITH

Toranj is one of my favourite restaurants in all of Edinburgh, and it's the only authentically Persian one. I discovered it by accident years ago. It's easy to miss, as it's situated below a hotel. Toranj is owned by a lovely Iranian family, and the menu has every traditional Iranian dish you can think of. They have handmade dolma that will literally melt in your mouth, and one of the best Fesenjoon I have tasted. Because it's so hidden away, it's often quiet and has free tables, so it's fitting for both families, friends, and date nights. Don't miss out on their saffron pistachio ice-cream; it's divine.

36. FROM MEXICO WITH LOVE

Another type of cuisine that has gained popularity amongst Scottish people in recent years is Mexican food. You'll easily find chains like Bar Burrito or Taco Mazama around the centre. For more authentic Mexican food, try El Cartel, who specialises in street food, tequila, and margaritas. Topolabamba and Viva Mexico are also popular amongst locals. Topolabamba often has good lunch deals and gives discounts to students, and their frozen margaritas are so good. Viva Mexico has maybe the best Mexican food I've ever tried, but for years the staff was well known for being pretty rude.

37. DESSERTS

Once, I went on a dessert road trip with my friend. We looked up all the best dessert places and spent two days trying all of them. The point of this anecdote is to emphasize that I love desserts and always stay up to date with new places opening. So let's move on from proper food and enter the realm of sugar.

38. CAKES, CAKES, CAKES

I have already mentioned a few cafés that have got a good cake selection. The one worth bringing up yet again is Mimi's. Mimi's has won awards for their cakes, and for a good reason.

A place to try is Artisan Cheesecake. They only sell cheesecake, but they have several mouth-watering kinds each day, and they top them with the most amazing toppings.

Café Konj is a little street café that sells cakes and pastries inspired by Iranian flavours. The owner is lovely, and she will happily help you choose the best sweet thing for you.

Patisserie Valerie is a French patisserie inspired cake chain. They sell some lighter food but are really known for the cakes and cake slices. They're also very affordable and often have offers on.

In spite of its name, The Stockbridge Kitchen serves delicious cakes. It's a tiny café that sells all kinds of sweet treats. In the Stockbridge part of the city, it might be a hike depending on where you're based. Still, the surroundings are astoundingly gorgeous, and the whole area is very walking friendly.

39. CUCKOO'S NEST

Cupcakes are an ever so popular dessert. But in my opinion, they often look pretty but are taste-wise pretty bland. An exception to this is The Cuckoo's Nest. They only do cupcakes, to indulge in their café with a hot drink, or for takeaway and delivery. Their flavours change every season, and the cupcakes are moist, flavourful, and anything but boring.

40. ICE-CREAM

In Edinburgh, you'll be able to find several local ice-cream makers. The most famous one is probably St Luca. Their ice cream can also be bought in tubs from shops, but if you want to experience their full assortment, you'll need to go to their café in Morningside.

Mary's Milk bar is another popular choice by locals and tourists alike. They have a few flavours each day and can be enjoyed scooped or as milkshakes. Sometimes they have the strangest flavour combinations, but every time the ice-cream is freshly made, soft, and delicious.

Gelato has had a recent upswing, and there are now several established gelato places. Artisan Gelato on Cockburn street makes all their ice-cream on location. They have various flavors, but in difference to Mary's Milk Bar, they are more traditional and less experimental. Their gelato is a welcome break if it's a warm day or if you've been walking around for hours.

But my favourite place any day of the week is Smoov. In addition to their super tasty, freshly made gelato, they have the best goddamn waffles around –

and they're all gluten-free! Smoov is a place of indulgence, so you'll fail to find anything healthy on their menu. They also have various types of coffee, milkshakes, and one or two savoury waffles.

41. THE WAFFLE PLACE

Speaking of waffles, The Waffle Place serves Asian bubble waffles. They also do some Asian dishes like bao and sushi, but we go there for the waffles. Served with a variety of toppings, they're an indulgent treat indeed. My friends and I love to there because it's also a perfect place to stay for a couple of hours.

42. DEDICATED TO DESSERT

Somewhat out of the city centre lies Kaspa's. This place is dedicated to desserts. It's literally all they sell. Everything from sweet pancakes and waffles to scoops of cookie dough and milkshakes – Kaspa's has it all. Since the location is a little off depending on where you're staying – it's in Gorgie – a great tip is to get it delivered. They're also open until late at night, making it ideal for a late-night treat to calm that sweet tooth.

43. BEVVIES

But what to do when you've eaten to heart's content? Drink, of course! Everyone knows about Scottish Whisky. But did you know that the United Kingdom is the most extensive gin making country in the world and that 80% of it is made in Scotland? Edinburgh alone is home to six gin distilleries, two whiskey distilleries, and several beer breweries.

44. A NOT SO TYPICAL BEER

Innis & Gunn is an Edinburgh local beer brand. For a long time, you were only able to buy their different drafts, cans, and bottles at various pubs and in shops. The brand is most known for letting its various beers mature in oak, rum, or whisky barrels. They also have a couple of different IPAs.

These days, Innes & Gun have their own brewery taproom in the centre of the city. Here you can try all of their different kinds of beers, and they also have a pretty extensive food menu. It's usually quiet during the days, making it perfect for families. At night it gets rowdier and is more suitable for friend groups.

45. SCOTLAND LOVES LOCAL

Brewdog is another popular Scottish beer brand, and just like Innes & Gunn, they have opened up their own brewery taproom. They are actually right across the road from each other, so you can easily go between the two if your goal is to try as many beers as possible. Brewdog serves food as well and has especially tasty burgers. My favourite beer of there is their Elvis Juice, a fruity IPA.

46. FOR THOSE WANTING TO TRY SOMETHING NEW

If you don't want to lock yourself down to one beer brand, my best tip is the Hanging Bat. Hanging Bat is a small pub with comfortable seating, perfect for a date, to take your mum, or to meet up with friends. Their beer menu changes frequently, and they have several guest taps each month. The staff is knowledgeable and helpful and are happy to let you sample the beers before buying. All of my really great beer experiences have happened here, and it's also thanks to them that my mother now enjoys beer.

47. GIN, GIN, GIN

As previously mentioned, Edinburgh has six gin distilleries alone, and together with all other distilleries around Scotland, there's an infinity to drink through. I would recommend everyone to take a trip to The Jolly Botanist, which is a pub that has hundreds of different gins. They have a gin menu, where you can choose your gin and perfect tonic, and the staff is also happy to help with any questions.

48. VISIT A DISTILLERY

Another great tip is to visit a gin distillery. Edinburgh Gin, Pickering's, and Holyrood Distillery all offer gin tastings and tours and are located within the city centre. For a more unique experience, book a tour at the Old Curiosity Gin. Their distillery is about forty minutes from the city centre by bus. Their gins are interesting herbal combinations, and at their distillery, they grow all of their herbs. If you're curious about it but don't drink gin, they also do tea tastings.

49. WHAT ABOUT THE WHISKY?

Whisky is a drink that you'll either love or hate. The Scottish single malts have little in common with drinks such as bourbon or American whisky. Scottish whisky varies immensely in flavour and intensity depending on where in Scotland it has been distilled. If you're a whisky lover, I would absolutely recommend going on a distillery trip. You can do this independently or as part of a tour.

If you're unable or unwilling to leave Edinburgh during your stay, don't fret! There's still plenty of whiskies to enjoy. Several pubs and establishments have hundreds of different whiskies, and the staff are well educated in them. There's also The Scotch Whisky Experience at the very top of the Royal Mile. They offer tastings and tours and are the ultimate activity for any whiskey lover.

50. WHAT TO TAKE BACK HOME

Every year, without failure, my dad asks me to bring back a bottle of whisky for him. My mother asks for gin. My sister asks for tea. There are so many tasty treats in Scotland and Edinburgh that you'll never be at a loss for things to bring back as gifts – or for yourself.

If you're running out of space in your suitcase, it's handy to know that many of the gin and whisky shops in town can send your purchases to your home address. The Edinburgh Airport has a good assortment of both whiskey and local gin. The price is about the same as in the city, so that's another option.

Traditional Scottish sweets like teacakes, caramel logs, and tablet are all widely available in shops, souvenir places, gourmet food places, and at the airport. They're not necessarily popular with foreigners but are well-loved by locals.

BONUS TIPS

BONUS TIP 1.

If you want to try eating at fine dining places but are travelling on a budget, considering planning your meals to slightly before traditional dinner time. Many restaurants have great lunch offers, and some have reduced prices just before closing. Pretty much all of the Michelin-star rated restaurants in the city offer a set lunch menu, which is of outstanding value and will save you a lot of money compared to if you book a table for dinner.

BONUS TIP 2.

Edinburgh is the home to several pop-up bars and themed establishments. Panda and Sons is a bar that's hidden behind a fake bookshelf in a barbershop. Pop-Up Geeks feature themes such as Harry Potter and Game of Thrones, and everything from the décor to the drinks will be inspired by the current theme. So if you're looking for an experience as much as a place to eat and drink, consider looking them up.

BONUS TIP 3.

Deep-fried Mars bars weren't on the list because I would never actually recommend anyone to try them. They are sickly sweet and fatty, and since most chippy's will use the same friers as for their other dishes, it can have a sub taste of fish. But they are somewhat of a Scottish legend and cost nearly nothing. If you do want to try one, you can get it from pretty much any chippy shop, but they do say that Clam Shell on the Royal Mile makes a decent one.

BONUS TIP 4.

In addition to that, it is worth noting that late night food places tend to serve kebabs, pizzas, and fish and chips. If you're hungry for kebab, the best you can get is Shawarma King up on Leven Street. Further down is German Doner Kebab, an international chain, but their food is of really high quality.

BONUS TIP 5.

Scotland is home to much of the world's finest wool and cashmere, and you'll notice that shops sell it everywhere. While many of the places are directly aimed at tourists, there are some, like Johnston of Elgin, that have made high quality goods in Scotland for generations. If you're looking for gifts or something for yourself, don't miss out on getting either a lambswool or cashmere scarf.

BONUS TIP 6.

Edinburgh is home to the world's biggest arts and culture festival – The Fringe. Throughout the whole month of August, the city is packed with music, arts, theatre, and anything you can think of. But it's also packed with tourists, and therefore becomes the most expensive month of the year to stay. So unless you want to come to visit specifically because of the Fringe, consider visiting another time of the year.

BONUS TIP 7.

In addition to the Fringe, Edinburgh has several festivals or events dedicated to food and drinks each year. For example, the Big Big Gin Festival, which runs over several days, usually in April. There's also the Cheese Festival, selling everything cheesy you can imagine. Street food is an ever-popular concept. There are often street food festivals in various parts of the city, particularly on weekends and in summer.

BONUS TIP 8.

The weather is fickle in Scotland. One minute it may be sunny, the next it'll rain cats and dogs. No matter the season, always be prepared for sudden changes and carry an umbrella with you. Still, there are some seasons during which it might be more pleasant to visit. The best months are late spring, April-May. Autumn can is often long and pretty mild, so anytime between September-November can be either a hit or miss. The worst weather is generally in January and February, but the tickets are also the cheapest.

BONUS TIP 9.

Overall, Edinburgh is suitable for a family vacation. There's plenty of activities that both kids and adults will enjoy, and most places have children's prices. What's worth knowing is that you're allowed to bring children with you into the pub, but they will have to leave before either 8PM or 10PM, depending on the venue. So if you're looking to get some pub food, it might be worth considering lunch rather than dinner.

BONUS TIP 10.

Little needs to be said about Edinburgh's cultural heritage. The whole city is like a postcard and is the inspiration for places like Diagonal Alley from Harry Potter. Many old buildings are in excellent condition, and it's possible to visit, or even stay in some of them. If you're interested in history and what it was like to live back in the day, don't miss out on attractions such as Real Mary King's Close or Gladstone Land.

BONUS TIP 11.

Old cities are filled with ghosts, or so they say. Edinburgh is sometimes referred to as one of the most haunted places in Europe. The city has a dark history, with serial killers, witch hunts, and poor people being forced to live underground. The best way to learn about the ghouls and spirits of the city is to go on a ghost tour. Most of these tours are walking tours that will take you through specific parts of the city and talk about what's happened there. There's also a ghost bus for those less inclined to walk, where you only occasionally stop and stroll for a bit. I would definitely recommend booking a tour that will take you down into Edinburgh's vaults underneath Southbridge.

TOP REASONS TO BOOK THIS TRIP

If all of the above tips haven't already convinced you that Edinburgh should be your next travel destination, here are a couple more.

If you want the experience of a big city, with lots of shopping, food, activities, and history – but also enjoy the benefit of being able to walk everywhere, Edinburgh is the perfect destination. The old is mixed with the new, breathtaking views, and you're never far from a green area. You can climb up the extinct volcano Arthur's seat in the morning and later in the afternoon do luxury shopping at Harvey Nichols. While Scotland is known for its bad weather and sudden changes, you're never far from a shelter in Edinburgh. At the right time of year, the climate is perfect for outdoor exploring.

Edinburgh is budget friendly. You can get cheap tickets to Edinburgh from most European cities. If you go off-season, you can find tickets for nearly nothing. There's plenty of accommodation, everything from fancy hotels to bed and breakfasts, hostels, to

61

Airbnb's in someone's home. The city is nowhere near as expensive as London, and all accommodation generally has a high standard. You can always find cheap eats, and there's plenty of public spaces where one can hang out for free.

Museums are free. Most museums are owned by the government or the council, and there's no admission. Some exceptions can apply for temporary exhibitions. The Royal Mile alone hosts four museums. The Writers' Museum, The Museum of Childhood, Edinburgh Museum, and People's Story. National Museum of Scotland has an array of items, including Dolly the Sheep. The National Gallery, the Modern Gallery, and the Portrait Gallery are all also free for visitors.

An exception to this is The Surgeon's Hall Museum – a museum dedicated to the history of medicine and surgery. Not for the faint of heart, but if you're into the macabre, it's totally worth the admission price. On display is everything from tumours to limbs and a dental collection, as well as a pocketbook made from the skin of infamous murderer William Burke.

Throughout the year, Edinburgh hosts numerous cultural events. The concert hall Usher Hall used to only have classical music performances. Still, in recent years they have been hosts to various world-famous artists, and they also do film screenings with live orchestras. Tickets can be pricey, but there are various concessions and sometimes discounts if you book last minute.

On each side of Usher Hall lies Traverse Theatre and Lyceum Theatre. Traverse tends to put up smaller productions by up-and-coming playwriters. You also have Festival Theatre, the Playhouse and King's Theatre. All of the venues have packed programmes, and many shows are very affordable.

If you love music, you'll be glad to know that pubs tend to have live music several nights a week. There's something for everyone – from jazz to folk music.

If this still isn't enough, Glasgow is only a forty-minute train journey, or an hour on the bus, away from Edinburgh. Services run regularly through the day and night, and many people commute on a daily basis. All real big music events take place in Glasgow, as they have massive arenas such as the SSE Hydro. Some of the artists that have performed there are Beyoncé, Prince, Lady Gaga, Ed Sheeran, and Elton John.

Eat Like a Local

*'I always feel that when I come
to Edinburgh, in many ways I am
coming home.'*

– Alan Rickman

READ OTHER BOOKS BY CZYK PUBLISHING

Eat Like a Local United States Cities & Towns

Eat Like a Local United States

Eat Like a Local- Oklahoma: Oklahoma Food Guide

Eat Like a Local- North Carolina: North Carolina Food Guide

Eat Like a Local- New York City: New York City Food Guide

Children's Book: Charlie the Cavalier Travels the World by Lisa Rusczyk

---

Eat Like a Local

Follow *Eat Like a Local on* Amazon.
Join our mailing list for new books

http://bit.ly/EatLikeaLocalbooks

CZYKPublishing.com

Printed in Great Britain
by Amazon